Celeste Onorati

YOU ARE YOU

Your guide to Freedom from Stress

Buenos Books America

All rights reserved.
Copyright © 2005 by Celeste Onorati

Edited by Jerome Leonardi
Cover photographed by Aimee VanWettering

No part of this book may be reproduced, stored in a retrieval system, or transmitted by any means, electronic, mechanical, photocopying, recording, or otherwise, without written permission from the author.

Dustjacket hardcover
ISBN: 978-1-932848-37-3

Other editions available:
ISBN: 9781932848267 (PAPERBACK)
ISBN: 9781932848274 (E-BOOK)

BUENOS BOOKS AMERICA
Second U.S. printing 2007
info@BuenosBooks.us
http://www.buenosbooks.us

CONVENIENT WAY TO CONTACT BUENOS BOOKS AMERICA

E-MAIL info@buenosbooks.us

for

Jonathan & Aimee

with love

"This above all: to thine own self be true".

William Shakespeare-*Hamlet (Act I, scene III)*

Had it not been for You

I would not know who I am.

It was through you that I was able

to awaken to the understanding

That You are You.

You taught me that the most wonderful

quality to possess is the awareness of our

nature – good and bad, in that moment that

we all share…

for this I am grateful.

Celeste

CONTENTS

Chapter 1
What is Living in the Moment?......................1

Chapter 2
Heredity, Environment & Character................17

Chapter 3
The Mind...39

Chapter 4
Definitions of the Mind............................47

Chapter 5
The Nature of Duality..............................63

Chapter 6
Relationships...69

Conclusion
Staying On Track....................................77

Foreward

Live in the moment. Let it go.

Reality. Duality. Listen. Energy. Simple.

These words came tough to me. I laughed. I cried. I was angry. I was depressed. I was afraid. How could someone come to me and tell me to just let it go? To me, it was just too many emotions to just set free like a handful of balloons. But it was just what I did. I met Celeste when I was in my early twenties. I admired life in her eyes and her presence around people was unprecedented. I needed to know what it was that made this woman so powerful. Powerful was the only way to describe this woman's presence. I was about find out how powerful she really is.

Do you understand what I am telling you? The infamous line Celeste had for me after each little session she and I had. In the beginning she related her teachings to real world situations and then slowly went beyond reality. Celeste showed me the true meaning of reality. Reality is what you make it to be as a person, as an individual, with your own thoughts and feelings. "You have to take the good with the bad..." Sound familiar? You and I live this everyday but I truly believe that without this duality of life, there would be no true appreciation for living in the moment. Night and Day. Happy and Sad. Man and Woman. Sun and Moon. Coincidence that the very components of life we are made up have their own duality about them. Life was created to have duality. How do you find this balance? I realized I have found balance when I was able to see that even though the moon and sun are two total different aspects of creation that could not be more opposite yet one shining off the other makes them beautiful together. That beauty is the balance they have.

Celeste has always had an open door for everyone. Always ready and willing to unleash what you already have inside you dying to get out. I equate it to learning to ride a bike. She gives you the bike, the helmet and she stands behinds you and pushes. Anyone learning to ride a bike knows that you have to have great trust in the person behind you to make sure they will be there to guide you if you go down. It's that very trust that you will learn will grow in your own ability. You learned that after awhile you ride all by yourself and the person running behind you guiding you isn't there anymore and you didn't even know it. Believe in yourself and your ability to make a difference in your own life. You will leave a big impression on people that want to know how you do that. Celeste has taught me to live in the moment and keep it simple."

Doug Maresca

Author's Preface

This book contains a number of ideas that will improve our understanding of the basic human being. I believe that anyone can say that they still have many questions concerning who am I? Why am I here? What is this life all about? What are the answers or keys to a successful, happy life?

If I ask some people these questions and discuss these topics, they may say that they have the answers. Every human being on this planet has a path that they will follow. If the path that they choose works for them, then say no more; if it works and happiness is found, then that is all that matters.

The information contained in this book is the answers to many questions that I have always asked and searched for. It was my path to finding out how to be truly happy and live a life that is in harmony to our human nature.

The many problems and difficult situations that we encounter in life are what I write about. This book has to be read with an open mind and with the understanding that this is what I have learned and these are the keys that opened my awareness to living a healthy and happy life.

Everyone is capable of improvement; no one, not even I would ever say that I have all the knowledge in the world; that would be ignorant. Everyday I learn something new. It is when you have the wisdom to know this that you evolve to a higher state of being.

The reader should realize that this knowledge comes from my experiences that I am sharing.

And if by reading this text you should awaken to these possibilities, then know that you have done it on your own, for yourself, by yourself.

"Every beauty which is seen here below by persons of perception resemble more than anything else that celestial source from which we all are come...."

-Michelangelo (1475-1564)

It is to seek with effort, each person, on your own, for yourself by yourself.

---Celeste Onorati

INTRODUCTION

Living in the Moment- This is knowledge that I acquired after many years of searching for the purpose of my own existence. *Living in the Moment* is the understanding that I have reached through this search for knowledge. I continue to live by this understanding as my journey through life progresses. In the last ten years I have discussed and shared this understanding with many people.

What you will gain from this knowledge is a better understanding of yourself. *Living in the Moment* will allow you to become more productive and more creative.

This understanding allows you to maintain a sense of calmness in life, even when things seem intense and hectic. *Living in the Moment* is a very healthy way to live.

Our world is changing very rapidly. The technology that exists today gives us the ability to learn, listen, observe, and act. In this ever-changing world one can do these things conveniently from home, or thousands of miles away from home.

Due to this highly advanced technology, many truths in life are unfolding. Nothing seems to be hidden any longer. One can gain information from all over the world in seconds. It can be accessed via telephone, computer, television, and or radio. So what makes you think that it can't take seconds to learn information about yourself just as quickly? Recognize how far we have come as people. Our progress can be accredited to our intelligence and drive as human beings. I'm saying take advantage of this information. Wake up! Understand that you can gain awareness about yourself and the world you live in right now. Everyone has access to the knowledge that is overflowing in the world as well as the knowledge that lives within.

People are exposed to an excess of information and activity in the world everyday. At times this can be overwhelming. All things in life happen simply because we are, "living our lives." However, simply living our lives too often becomes stressful. In order to decrease the effects of stress, it is necessary to first gain an understanding of how stress works in our life. Then we may become aware of how to deal with it. Only then will you gain the freedom to live your life peacefully

Now is the time for us to begin to have a better understanding of who we truly are. I have accomplished this understanding by learning how to *Live in the Moment*.

It is something that can be understood quickly, without wasting any more time.

The body cannot function in a healthy way if the mind is not at ease with the body. You and only you can create this healthy mind set. The understanding of *Living in the Moment* becomes apparent to you and those around you as you begin to share it, (in most cases) without even knowing that you're doing it. Your peacefulness as well as your confidence becomes so obvious that those around you want to learn from you and obtain those qualities as well.

The understanding that I live with now allows me to share it; and furthermore, I encourage you to find it for yourself. The information that leads to this understanding is there. It's within you. It is yours; you simply have to want it. It enables you to understand yourself and others. It gives you the ability to stay focused, to enjoy your life, and to live with the understanding of the word stress. The awareness you will gain allows you to remain young, healthy, happy, and relieved.

Whatever you take or leave from this journey, know that it is yours…
Celeste

Chapter 1

What is Living in the Moment?

When people ask me what I do, I tell them. I teach people how to *Live in the Moment*.

Living in the Moment means coming back to the here and now. It means waking up and realizing where you are this very unique moment and how to stay on track in this moment for a more productive life.

In order to understand living in the moment, you have to understand the conscious mind. Without the conscious mind, it won't matter if you're *Living in the Moment*; it only means that you are no longer alive.

The conscious mind is what has to be trained in order to understand *Living in the Moment*. You will start living your life in a more peaceful and healthy way.

In this book I will teach you how to understand your mind. I will teach you how to enjoy a richer more productive life just by understanding how the mind works. This is a book that is cards on the table, and I will tell you point blank, exactly how the mind works. It is not that hard to understand how it works. It just takes work, and only you can make that work. Once you understand this, you will kick up your heels and rejoice. You will wonder why it took you so long to understand something that you already knew existed deep inside of you. It is a knowing and a place of comfort that already exists.

And it's just a matter of getting that key and opening up the door and understanding how and why we do the things that we do. When you understand this your levels of stress drop dramatically. What could be better than that? Gaining the confidence and the strength to live each day with the understanding that this is your life and only you have the control to make it good or bad.

So stop being afraid of who you really are and learn about yourself!

A friend asked me to be more specific about living in the moment. He asked,

Celeste - I just visited your web site. Question - have you been able to "reach" people and get them to *Live in the Moment* for each moment in the day when they are faced with planning for the next day (week or month) and are following up for things that should have happened yesterday (or last week/month)?

Of course I am able to reach people, once the understanding is there. Every day we are faced with planning for the next day; what you have to remember is that at that moment, when you are planning, that is the moment. Tomorrow will come when that moment arises that you have already planned for, so make the plan and wait to see it unfold when it gets there. Do what you have to do in the moment, tomorrow is another day.

The course of action that you spend making plans for today can change tomorrow. Then doesn't that become yesterday's plan? Move with your life to what is happening in this moment. To live with expectations of tomorrow brings up feelings of not knowing, anything we do not know, is what we fear. When you look back at yesterday's plan you see that it can change. So why spend time thinking about it, go on with your life in this moment. You start to lose your focus when you think forward or backward. Yes, most times we will do this; it is becoming aware of this forward/backward thinking and where the mind likes to go, then return to the moment and return to what it was that you were doing. The conscious mind likes to drift. It is always getting distracted. It constantly plays in thoughts of yesterday or tomorrow. When you start to witness the way the mind gets distracted you will start to understand how the mind works.

The sub-conscious mind stores all of your past information, while the super-conscious mind is your intelligence. This super-conscious mind can't seem to get in contact with you, because the small conscious mind is playing all by itself. The small mind is making up all kinds of scenarios that don't even exist. It plays on the fears of not knowing. It is the unruly child who will not listen. The superconscious mind, intelligence, is always there for you; you just have to be more aware of it and listen to it. It is where your intuition comes from; it is where all of our intelligence resides. The unconscious mind is what it is, the sleep/dream/coma state; you have no awareness, no control. You owe it to yourself to become more aware of the intelligent mind. It is yours; you own it, so start using it. The more you become aware of the conscious mind drifting and not staying in the now, the more you start to understand the time that you waste getting stuck in thinking forward or backward.

An athlete on the playing field knows this understanding. If their mind starts to wander forward or backward they cannot achieve their focus in the game. The athlete needs to remain in the moment to reach their goals. If not, they do not play their game to the ultimate level that they can achieve. Every athlete knows this. An actor knows this when on stage or on film: he has to be in the moment with his character. A surgeon hopefully knows this when he is performing surgery. The list can go on. You have to be who you are at that moment and focus in that moment. It leaves no room to screw up, and it works with everything in life. We don't realize and we take for granted our abilities as human beings. When we utilize our five senses and become aware of them we start to see opportunities that are often missed. Why? Because we get too caught up in our fears of tomorrow and desires of yesterday, it's that simple! Start to let your attentions become unbroken, the distraction will finally give up the struggle, and will start to let you live your life in peace.

If you have a task to accomplish, do it! At that moment don't leave any gaps open for your focus to be broken. I see it all the time! I meet someone and start a conversation with him and I can feel his mind drift out of our conversation. Now, I can say that since I have learned these principals of watching the mind, I understand where I came from at one time and I felt as though I was cheating that person of giving him my utmost attention at that moment. I look at it now and say how rude… to not give my attention to someone who is speaking to me. It is a waste of energy and also not very good manners. When you understand this and you work with it, you will start to see how this happens to you with other people. Try it, have a conversation with someone and stay in the moment of that conversation and watch the other person and see if her mind is drifting or if she is in the moment with you. It is a lot of fun, and nine times out of ten, she is not. People do it all the time because they do not know how to stay focused and in the moment. It is only then that you will discover how the mind works with all of us. So try for a time, try to gather all your senses and take a look at the moment. Everything that is around you, see it, smell it, hear it, taste it, and feel it. It becomes the art of life. It is where all the magic in your life starts to unfold. I can relate it to a small child or even an animal. A small child lives in the moment, he wants what he wants at the moment. Yes, he knows what he desires but he doesn't let his mind get carried away with the future, if he is hungry he will tell you, if he wants your attention, he will tell you.

It is you that can't stay in the moment with him, because you are already conditioned to have your mind go somewhere else. Notice a small child, if there is one available and see what I am talking about. They rely on us to remain focused and guide them to a feeling of being loved and nourished. That is all that they ask for, nothing else. They work with the resources that they have in the moment.

Notice animals, why do you think that they run away from us? They can sense that we are not living in the moment. Why? Because they live there. If you sit quietly, observe and become aware of the moment, you will see that they can intuitively feel this. They are afraid of us; they can feel that our mind is not in tune with their being present and that our mind is somewhere else. They know this! They can sense if we are not in the same moment because that is how they get through life. In the moment, it does not matter to them.

It is nature and it is how we should strive to learn, through nature. It will show us everything we need to learn. We don't know when we are born and we don't know when we die. Everything in nature just comes and goes, and it is only for a short time. Understand how important it is to start and become aware of who you are and how you think. Start to watch your mind. Witness what goes on in your head. It's amazing because when you get it you start to see the same busy mind in other people, and you don't judge them so quickly, you start to understand why. It is so easy, start to understand this stuff and get your act together! Do it for yourself! When you live by this understanding, people will notice and want to learn from you. You start to become more relaxed and in tune with nature. Much more at peace and not so stressed out.

You have a more confident and positive outlook on life because you understand that you are the only one that controls how you think of things. No ONE can take this away from you; it cannot be touched, and it is not physical.

An Awareness of yourself is needed in order to feel more comfortable while you learn how to discover who you are and how to trust yourself. You start to remove the obstacles in your life and you watch the opportunities come forward; it is magical. As this process begins, stress levels start to change and begin to have more positive effects on the mind and body. One begins to understand the purpose of stress in life and the lessons it teaches us. Living in the moment allows us to notice these lessons and embrace them. The importance of mind-body connection can be further explained in the example of the August 31st, 2002 edition of *Scientific American*. The article focuses on this connection: "Nothing is more familiar than the mind. Yet the pilgrim in search of the sources and mechanisms behind the mind embarks on a journey into a strange and exotic landscape. In no particular order, what follows are the main problems facing those who seek the biological basis for the conscious mind. The first quandary involves the perspective one must adapt to study the conscious mind in relation to the brain in which we believe it originates. Anyone's body and brain are observable only to its owner. Multiple individuals confronted with the same body or brain can make the same observation of that body and brain, but no comparable direct third-person observation is possible for anyone's mind. The body and its brain are public, exposed external and unequivocally objective entities. The mind is a private, hidden, internal unequivocally subjective entity" [1]

Learn it, Live it and find it…then keep it. It is a knowing that we have, it just happens to get lost, most of the time because we don't trust our own intelligence. Start to use it, it's yours.

Chapter 2

Heredity, Environment & Character

On Heredity:

I was very relieved when I learned about this and understood it. When we are born we inherit the genes of our parents. What you inherit with your physical body is pretty much what you will go through in your life as far as having to deal with your health and looks. It is that simple. Your insides and outsides will resemble your creators/parents.

Fortunately today, we can easily have our physical bodies corrected. If you want a smaller nose, larger breasts, remove fat, have surgery to lose weight, have new hair, no problem, it can happen. Everyone has an option today to change what they are not comfortable with on their body. Reconstructive surgery is a big business. If you think that having something done to change your looks will make you feel better, then go ahead.

You don't have to go around any more feeling uncomfortable with the way you look. It can be changed. The technology today gives us the ability to do whatever it is that we are trying to achieve, <u>very quickly</u> and precise. People who were born with deformities or that have been in accidents can have corrective surgery. Watch the extreme makeover channels and you will see what I am talking about. In no time you can have your whole body reconstructed and look like a whole new person. If that is what you want, then do it! There is no need for obsessing and worrying about your physical state. If it takes changing how you look to feel better about yourself and to quiet the mind, then do it. If this will give you a more positive attitude, then go for it. It is the positive attitude in life that brings you closer to feeling good about who you are. I have heard so many stories of young girls in their teens that have to deal with their mothers telling them all the time that they are fat. Can you imagine that! Where is the positive reinforcement for these girls?

In today's society it is not socially acceptable to look any other way. Even if it means throwing up your food, can you imagine that? Fortunately, we can do something about it. I don't recommend throwing up your food; that is not a safe or healthy way to drop weight, that makes no sense at all. Whatever happened to the healthy way of exercising? Or watching what you eat? If you know that being overweight runs in your family then watch what you eat. Most of the time eating foods that are not healthy for you can also make you lazy and depressed. You eat, don't exercise and then you lie around and sleep. Whose fault is that? So it is simple, if you don't like the way you look, then do something about it, there are so many options today. No excuses.

On Environment:

Oh, this is the good one! One that made me feel much better after I realized all about the environment I was raised in, you will also.

It doesn't matter who raises you, did you hear that? You could have been given up by your parents as a child and someone else raised you. It doesn't matter who raises you, did you hear that again?

It is your environment that influences how and why you do the things that you do. Should I say it again? This is so important, it is your environment that influences how and why you do the things that you do!!! Get it into your head and remember it.

We will start from the moment you took your first breath. That would be consciousness. Without consciousness you do not exist. Lets look at this in a way that everyone can relate; let's say to a video tape, DVD anything that is going to record your life. So we say that you come into this life with a recorder that is going to keep track of all the events in your life, every second. How's that? The minute you take that first breath that tape starts to play. Everything that happens in the start of your life gets recorded. Everything gets stored in your subconscious, and you can play it back anytime you want, you control the functions of play, stop, fast forward, rewind record and pause. Only you have access to this remote control, it's invisible, so let's say that the remote control is your intelligence or super-conscious mind. Stay with me. You can hit play (consciousness) or stop (live in the moment-super-consciousness), fast forward (fear of the unknown, it has not happened yet), rewind (subconscious desire-living in the past) record (live in the moment-super-consciousness) and pause (unconscious sleep/dream/coma). This is what I have learned and remember to live by, understand it. You are the music in your own life; you are the actor in your own movie. You are the instrument that observes and controls how you want to live your life. You are what you eat, physically and mentally. Remember that you are brought into an environment that you will learn from. What you learn is what you are shown. It is not who you are. There will come a time when you are able to see yourself as your own individual. As a young child you don't have any control or say in your development. You will be raised by the standards that were instilled, most of the time by your caretakers. You can be raised in a household of wealth or poverty, educated or non-educated, it doesn't matter. What matters is where your caretakers/parents heads were at, during your stages of development. As a young child you look to these caretaker/parents to try and figure out how to get around in life. You are hoping most of the time that they can get their heads out of their asses. All the time you are observing where their minds are. Usually they are caught up in their fears and desires, for they too are searching, not even knowing what it is that they are looking for. They try to find it in anything that they think will bring happiness outside of themselves. When it is right within them, do they know this? Of course not. They still think that all the material things in life will give them the happiness that they are looking for. Unfortunately that is what we all do. The material things can come and go. Remember the old saying: here today and gone tomorrow. When you understand that these material things are not permanent, and that nothing is permanent, you start to have a better understanding of who you are.

You don't take life for granted; you start to see the value of life and what it has given you. Then it doesn't matter how they treat you, you have the understanding of life, and all you become aware of is their behavior and what you are being taught. You can't blame them, but boy they will show you, whether you like it or not. Hopefully if they have the desire to understand this knowledge then everyone can work on it together. It is such a more positive way to live your life. So remember, if they are prejudice, you will learn that. If they are money hungry, you will learn that. If they are physical, you will learn that. If they are jealous, you will learn that. Everything that they experience on their journey during your years of development will be what you learn. Is this good or bad? It doesn't matter; you will be able to choose which path and what life you want to live once you are an adult. Your sub-conscious mind will store all of this information and you probably will think that you have to follow the pattern you were taught in order to feel close to home and be close to what is familiar. When you understand this, you will start to have an understanding and hopefully a compassion for these caretakers/parents that only do the best that they can, because that is what they were shown. It is a cycle that continues for as long as you let it. Only you have the awareness to recognize this and do something about it, for yourself. Otherwise you are just going to repeat this process again to your off-spring, and then not understand what it was that you did wrong. You will want to blame someone. There is no one to blame! Get your act together, you don't have to follow the path that you were shown, if you think that you have the most jealous mother in the world, stop talking about it, because if you are talking about it that just means that you are doing the same thing, (although you don't think that you are). Again, it feels comfortable to play there, because that is what you were shown. Here we go-- let's recap; if you were physically hit as a child, you will hit. If you were lied to, you will lie; if you were taught how to cheat, you will cheat. These are the things that you were taught and they feel comfortable because they were the tools that you subconsciously have come to know and use. In my case, because I was physically hit as a child, I kept telling myself that if I ever had children I would not follow that way of teaching, and I did not. I have witnessed children that were hit and guess what? They were always hitting other children. Why am I listing all the negative things? Because the negative things are what hold you back in life. The understanding of life is what I am getting at; it is the most important thing to become aware of. We are only here for a short period of time, we do not have to follow the patterns that we were taught. You can snap the hell out of it, and remember, so that when it is your time to bring another human being into this world, you are prepared to do so, and in so doing, try and keep the dysfunctional ways out of the picture. I have learned to accept what has been shown to me, and I can go on with my life in a way that has had a much more positive affect on my children. That was exactly what I was looking for, but it had to come through me first. I knew instinctively that what I exposed them to would have an affect on their lives for the future. I did not want to expose them to the negative experiences that I was taught or that I was living. I wanted for them the experiences of living in a positive state of awareness so that they could live their lives and continue their journey in this life with the understanding and confidence of knowing that they create all and any obstacle that comes their way. I have realized that they were going to learn this and I needed to expose them to this understanding of life. This was my job as a caretaker/parent. Why in the world would I want to put another dysfunctional being on this earth? I had to get my act together. We create and teach our children everything that they know. Why would I want them to live in a world of chaos, when I could teach them how chaos is created and what you need to do to overcome and not create chaos within the self. The self is the only place where chaos resides. Believe me; I still have experiences that are good and bad however the difference is that I do not get attached to any one experience. I continue to live my life and witness the events around me. I don't worry about what tomorrow may or may not bring. I have a better understanding of stress and how it affects me physically and mentally. I have become more aware of my surroundings. I adjust to situations and I am socially comfortable. My children witness this way of living. They are respectful because they have found the respect within themselves. They are aware that all knowledge that is gained is taught by someone else and that the wisdom to understand this comes from within.

On Character:

Everything that you think you are, you are not. This one was a little difficult for me to understand at first. How could I not be who I thought I was?

When I looked in the mirror I saw me, how I physically looked. I would wake up in the morning and see myself one way and then I would take my shower and dress and see myself another way. I would start my day always thinking that I would have to act and present myself one way and to put on a personality and carry my ego around with me, to be this way or that way and try to find comfort with it. I felt that who I was on the inside was not who I was on the outside. It wasn't until I finally understood through all of my searching and investigating that I realized, I am not the physical body, I am much more than that. My true character is the essence of pure intelligence. I am the doer of all my actions. I am who I am… my character is me. I learned that once I got rid of that ego, personality, the false me, that my life started to change. My ego, personality, was not who I really was. It's sort of like the car you drive; it is what people see when they see you. So I knew that what I learned meant that I had to use my own intelligence to guide me and help me feel comfortable with the real me and not to think anymore that I had to impress anyone with what I learned to believe was not the real me, not my real character. I did not have to do or think any way that was not familiar to me or what was taught to me. I was free to be comfortable with me and not be bound by what someone else thought. I realized that our body comes and goes, just like everything else in life, but that the essence and intelligence of who I am would always be around. We come and we go physically, and we are only here for a short period of time. Why would I want to waste this time and be caught up in being someone I wasn't? I like me. The most powerful thing to know is that I am beyond the physical; I am the intelligence beyond anything that I can physically touch. So what makes you think that anything or anyone can harm you? It is just not so. This is true with everything that arises in your life; no one can come in to you and change the power that you have within you. No disease, no person, no one. Of course, the disease may have already taken over your physical body, but it cannot take over your intelligence. It is that simple, you are the only one who can allow that to happen. When it is your time to go, and leave this earth, you will go. You didn't know when you were born and you don't know when you will die. What you do know is what you have forgotten, and that is your intelligence as a human being and your ability to use this intelligence at all times. You and only you have the power to heal yourself or make yourself stay sick. Nothing can take you over, unless you allow it. The mind can be altered or changed through mind altering substances. Some of these substances can chemically alter your brain and destroy it. They take away your character. They put you in a place where you have no control over your intelligence. What are these mind altering substances? You can start with tobacco, caffeine, alcohol, drugs, anything that can stimulate or change the chemicals in the brain, for a second or for an hour, or for days. These substances are all available to us, anytime and anywhere, by prescription, legally or illegally. All of these substances that you take are a temporary fix; they are not permanent. They alter who you are, they change your character, they put you outside of yourself you loose who you are. It all becomes a distortion of your character. Yes, there are always going to be times in your life where you need help in trying to get through tough situations; we all go through it. But these substances don't change anything; they temporarily alter your mood for a period of time. I do say thank goodness for some of the prescription drugs that are out there. There are some people that just can't seem to get through the tough situations and they need a boost to feel more relaxed and calm. Take anti-depressants for example. This is a prescription drug that changes the chemical patterns of the brain. Are there some people that definitely need to be on them? Of course, because of a genetic chemical imbalance. However, there are far too many people taking these drugs today who are not getting the proper therapy to see if they really need to be on them. Anti-depressants are not a quick fix and at times they can do more harm than good, depending on your particular case or problem... just look at the side effects. One danger is the direct link between suicide and violent behavior. There is a lack of full understanding about how anti-depressants and depression affect the brain. Read about the studies that are being done. Also, start to read more about the mind-body connection, there are so many articles.

What is the attraction to wanting to feel outside of ourselves? Why do we want to change who we are? To be someone we are not? What is it that we are looking for that we can't change or achieve on our own? What is it that you can't face? What is it that you can't deal with? What makes you so afraid? Think about it, understand it, and use your intelligence.

Chapter 3
The Mind

It's yours.
You control it. You own it.

It's not a physical thing, no one can touch it.

The mind thinks, they are your thoughts, no one can tell you how to think. As I was writing this chapter, my son was reading *Harry Potter*. He was so excited to share what he was reading in that moment.

As quoted in *Harry Potter and the Order of the Phoenix*, *"the mind is not a book, to be opened at will and examined at leisure. Thoughts are not etched on the inside of skulls, to be pursued by any invader. The mind is a complex and many layered thing."* [2]

You decide what mood you want to be in, good or bad. You decide how long you want to stay in that mood. Only you can change your mood, no one can do it for you.

The mind is thinking all the time. It's creating. It either thinks in the future, or it thinks in the past. When it is thinking in the future it creates fears, the fears of not knowing what will happen one minute from now, one month from now, or one year from now. When the mind thinks of the past, it creates desire. It desires something you have already experienced, and the experience is familiar, and you want to experience it again.
When the mind is not creating future or past, and it is engulfed with the here and now, it is the *Living in the Moment.*

When the mind drifts to the future or the past, it is normal. What I'm telling you is to **become aware of the mind drifting to the future and the past, watch where it just went. Then come back to where you were and what you were supposed to be doing.**

It is very simple. It just takes work. Be aware of how your mind works, you will be amazed.

I am not telling you that you have to live in the moment twenty-four seven. All I'm saying to you is that when you become aware of what living in the moment is you start to recognize how the busy mind works and how it creates unnecessary activity to take you away from your focus. The mind creates obstacles. When you gain the awareness of watching your mind, you start to understand how your mind works.

You and your mind create your own obstacles. Look, anyone can touch you physically! They cannot touch your mind! Nobody does anything to you. How can they? We are the highest beings on this planet. What makes you think that something or someone can come into your mind and control your thoughts? Take any scenario that you want, or better yet, I'll give one to you.

You just had an argument with someone, for whatever reason. It happened a minute ago. What most will do is play that scenario over and over again in their head. Yeah, everybody does it.

The only thing that this does is make you physically sick. The body can only handle so much of the stress that you're putting on it. You are the only one that can let that scenario go. Keep it in the past. Don't get attached to why it happened. It just did, it is a part of life. It's when the mind gets attached to these things that you can't move on and be productive with your life. You lose your focus. When you understand this, and when you watch this, the busy mind, and how it works you get a better understanding of how to chill out. Life is too short to waste your time dwelling on the past and thinking of the future, enjoy what you have right now, and chill out!

"Life is what happens while your busy making other plans."

John Lennon

Chapter 4

Definitions of the Mind

*W*hen we say the **MIND**, *what are we talking about?*

Webster's Dictionary definition of the mind says "consciousness considered as residing in the human brain manifested especially in thought, perception, feeling, will, memory and imagination".

When we say **UN-CONSCIOUS,** *what are we talking about?*

Webster's definition of unconsciousness says "you are completely lacking in awareness, as in a coma or deep sleep."

When we say **SUB-CONSCIOUS,** *what are we talking about?*

Webster's definition of subconscious says "Not wholly conscious but capable of being made conscious."

When we say **INTELLIGENCE,** *what are we talking about?*

Webster's definition of intelligence says "The capacity to acquire and apply knowledge. The faculty of thought and reason. Superior powers of mind."

When we say **CONSCIOUSNESS,** *what are we talking about?*

Webster's definition of consciousness says "it is a critical awareness of one's own identity and situation. It is the state or condition of being conscious."

And last but not least, the word **WISDOM**...

Webster's definition of wisdom says "Enlightened understanding of what is true or right, usually acquired through long experience, as distinguished from a partial or specialized knowledge."

See, I am making this easier for you already. I just saved you the trip of looking up all of these words. I believe sometimes we think we know what they mean, although it doesn't hurt to read them again.

We will be using these words throughout the content of this book. It is important for you to understand what they mean.
Just one more thing...

As I was putting this definitions list together, I realized that five of these words spelled one amazing word, and that word is MUSIC. What a coincidence!

"The wise musicians are those who play what they can master."

Duke Ellington

MUSIC=LIFE

Face the music... you are you.

The

    Mind

        Unconscious

            Subconscious

                Intelligence

                    Consciousness

Understanding this becomes **MUSIC** to your ears, with the **WISDOM** to acquire it!
You own it, it's yours

Music is everywhere; it is a part of nature. From the sound of the rain to a bird's song, everyone can hear or feel music. Every culture and every living creature in this world has their own music.

Music is understanding, whatever mood you're in music enhances it. Music is therapy. It has a way of connecting you to yourself.

How does living in the moment relate to music? Well, when you're listening to your favorite song, you are living in the moment. Focused in that moment, body soul and spirit, joined together to heal yourself.

Yes, I'm sitting here watching my neighbor come home from her food shopping. I recognize that she's playing loud music in her car and this makes her happy. I know that at the same time, I'm trying to get my thoughts together to continue talking to you about music, and how it affects people. As I am sitting here at the computer typing and I am looking at a section of a newspaper dated February 15, 2005. That was the day that I had spent with my dad in the hospital, before he passed away on February the 18th. And low and behold the section in the newspaper had an article on health and fitness and the title was: "Music in the operating room." The title states surgeons say it helps them concentrate.

"There are a lot of OR sounds that have no meaning for the operating surgeon" "says Butterfield, who works at the woman's plastic surgery Center Inc. in Cincinnati and is partial to old-school R&B. "It's almost like really loud white noise. Music takes away from the background noise that's too distracting." "The general consensus is the OR is a stressful place and music provides relaxation. *(OR abbreviation-Operating Room, Old school R&B abbreviation-Old School-Rhythm and Blues).*

There's plenty of research that says music is good for patients: It relieves stress, eases the perception of pain, even triggering memory in people with Alzheimer's."

"It's Sinatra, all the time, when Dr. Howard Melvin, an eye surgeon, is in the operating room."

"I need something relaxing. I do very intense surgery," he says.

Some days, Dr. Robert Bohinski wants to hear Mozart in the operating room. Other days, only *Guns 'N' Roses* will do.

"Sometimes it just depends on what team we have that day, whether it's an older team or a younger team," says Bohinski, a neurosurgeon. "Usually it's just a gut feeling."³

Music just does something to all of us and it doesn't matter what mood we are in; music just has a way of enhancing or altering it. It is the one thing that motivates your thoughts and keeps you in the moment that you are creating. It is the experience of that moment that plays with you and relates to you. Music talks to you and always has a way of understanding what you are feeling at that moment. Isn't it funny that when there are times that your mood is one way or another and you turn on some music and the song that is playing reminds you of what you are experiencing… it happens to all of us.

A friend and I were talking about this, and he explained his version of music and his spin on it with regards to feeling. At the same time another friend came in and started talking about this same experience that she went through just on her drive over to meet us. The conversation became an understanding of what we all feel happens to us when we have music in our lives. Music helps us all in so many ways. The kinds of music for every state of mind you are in; depressed, happy, sad, intellectual, it makes you feel sad or happy. Your state of mind goes along with every kind of music in life. Every person has her own kind of music. So if you are listening to country, rap, classical, rock, it doesn't matter; every artist will sing about it and relate it to their life. This friend also went on to tell me that he was watching late night with Conan O'Brien and one of his guests was Jamie Fox. He told me about the interview and said that this should be included in my book.

They were talking about making the movie *Ray* and Jamie, of course was playing Ray Charles, and Jamie had a chance to hang out with Ray Charles before he died. Fox and Ray were playing the piano together, and they were playing the blues and Fox missed a note. Ray Charles said to Jamie, "take time to find the right notes, the notes are right underneath your fingers." And Jamie explained that what Ray Charles really meant was that he was really relating this to life and music, and that in life, we know that the notes are there, we see the keys, we see the strings, we know what all the keys are and what the strings are, but we just need to find the right music to play.

So to conclude, find your own music and know that it all comes from you and understanding your own keys for living a happy life. With music there is a song to make you laugh, or a sad song to make you cry, one to make you reminisce or a song to keep you relaxed. Whatever it is there will always be a piece of music to go along with your state of mind. Any emotion you are holding on to will have a song to go with it. There are times when you break up with a boyfriend and you are on your way home and every song on the radio that is being played will have to do with the breakup that just occurred. Or maybe someone you loved has passed away and you hear a song that reminds you of him or her and in your heart you know that he or she are right there with you. Funny isn't it? It happens to all of us. Music will tell you what you need to hear, at that moment. Music is magical, it talks to us.

"Music produces a kind of pleasure which human nature cannot do without"

Confucius

Chapter 5

The Nature of Duality

We live in the world of Duality. Everything has its opposite. Night and day, good and bad, rich and poor, happy and sad, the list goes on and on. I came to understand this and it made me more aware of everything that takes place in our lives. You cannot have one without the other. In order to experience happiness you have to know sadness. It is that simple. What I have learned is that the attachment to either one will knock you off track and keep you out of balance. The balance in nature is understanding its opposite and intelligently accepting both. When you have this understanding you start to live your life in a more positive, productive way. So many times we complain about all the negative bad things in life. It is so much easier to see the bad because we start to feel very sorry for ourselves. Oh, Why ME? Poor ME! ...Get over it! The conscious mind loves to stay stuck in those negative places. It gives the conscious mind the fuel it needs to stay there and make you physically sick. The super-conscious mind (intelligence) knows the difference. It is very aware of how the conscious mind works. I have done it myself and know so many people that do the same thing, worry. If you had a bad day, you will keep recalling that day in your head, you will make everyone around you just as miserable as you. You know the saying "misery loves company." You will attract that type of energy everywhere you are, why because it works that way. You will stay angry, and you will attract angry. The minute you look at your thoughts and remove a bad day out of your head, you will get its opposite, Good day. Only you have the ability to choose which way you want to feel. Take notice next time you're driving to work and you're in a bad mood, you will attract every moron out there that is in your same mood. Talk about road rage!

Or you are in a hurry and you need to get somewhere fast, guess what? You are going to run into everyone that slows you down. (It is what you asked for; if you want to change that, do the opposite). If you want to stay healthy, think healthy, if you want to stay sick, think sick. You will always get what you want. It is your choice, only you can experience the nature of duality and only you can understand how it works. If you want to think yourself poor, stay poor, if you want to think yourself rich, get rich. Only you can make it happen. Everything in life will show you its opposite, DO NOT get stuck in either one. Let your life unfold and show you the wonderful things that you are here to experience. This is what life is all about. Whether the good times and the bad times, learn and move on. It does not change, only you can become aware and unattached to the events of duality that unfold in your mind, you are the only one that can change from one to the other.

"Follow your instincts. That's where true wisdom manifests itself."

Oprah Winfrey (1954 -)

Chapter 6

Relationships

"You are the people who are shaping a better world.
One of the secrets of inner peace is the practice of compassion."
-Dalai Lama (1935 -)

Oh Boy, where do we start? When you come into this life you start with relationship. Other words would be connection, involvement, friendship. We all have a relationship with someone in this lifetime, family, friends, classmates, co-workers... and the best one, your significant other. We all think that there is someone out there who will understand us or maybe someone who is just like us. Everyone searches for this connection; it is a part of our journey in life. You need to have relationships in order to understand yourself. Most of the time the hardest painful relationships are the ones that really make you learn more about yourself.

EXPECTATION. This word clearly explains relationships from the very start of your existence in this life. As a baby, you expect to be fed, listened to and loved. You intuitively expect that your caretakers will be available to you at all times. As we grow we continue to have expectations with every relationship that we are in. We want everything to be the way we want it to be. This is where the difficulties come from, expectation. We expect the other person to know exactly what it is that we want. If these expectations are not fulfilled, we automatically want to change that person. We become unhappy with the situation and we can't seem to figure out how the other person can't see these things that we expect. It becomes a vicious cycle that ends relationships sometimes for the dumbest things. You cannot expect your parents, relatives, friends, co-workers, boss, or anyone close to you to change. They are who they are and you are who you are. Who cares if they leave the toilet seat up or down, or they don't put the cap back on the toothpaste. We sometimes act like little babies, always crying because the other person doesn't see things the way that we want them to. It is our expectation, not theirs. Our lives change dramatically when we let go of these expectations. We no longer have to feel that someone else will make that difference in our lives. It starts with you, with your understanding of the other person. Let go of anything that you expect from someone else. Start to work on yourself and examine how you react to these situations. The only person you should be looking at changing is yourself. It takes a lot of effort just to work on your own stuff, start there, the changes are worth it.

DEADLINES. This is what makes people go nuts! Talk about stress. You hear a young girl at the age of 25 saying that her life is over because she has not accomplished anything yet that she had planned or hoped to. She should be married, she should have at least three kids, she should have been successful by now… isn't she nuts! What is the hurry? Why do we want things to happen so quickly? And if we don't we think that we are doomed.

ALONE. Here is a good one. We are raised in believing that we are not complete unless there is that special someone in our lives. Yet when we do find someone it is usually good when it starts. Why, because we hide behind our real selves. We never show the other person who we really are. When the real self comes out watch out! It is only when you move forward with the relationship that you start to see things in the other person that you are not happy with. And you want to change the other person but you can't so you will stay in it because you are afraid to be alone. You are used to the routine that you have built up with that person, whether it is good or bad. Oh sure you think that this is your "soul mate" or the "one." Are you kidding me? The only one that there is, is YOU. If you truly care that much about someone then don't expect, don't have deadlines and don't fear being alone. When you understand this then you will give yourself a chance to know yourself and the other person completely. Just as we come into this world by ourselves, we leave by ourselves, and it goes by very quickly.

"Follow your bliss."

-Joseph Campbell (1904-1987)

Conclusion

How to Stay on Track

The mind likes to drift...

Teach yourself to notice this when it does.

Watch the mind and where it just went.

Don't judge your thoughts!

Come back to the moment.

Open your eyes to what is around

you.

Notice everything.

Take the time to do this.

Observe what is happening in this moment.

If you are involved in a task, stay focused on the task.

If the mind starts to drift, come back to your task.

Learn to keep your mouth shut and observe.

Understand Duality.

Everything in nature is dual.

Remember, it was your environment and what you were taught.

You are the only one that can do this, for yourself.

Become the witness to your thoughts.

Watch Your Mind

Come back to the Moment

Live in the Moment

This book is your "key"

to understanding

Who You Are

You Are You!

Notes

[1] *Scientific American*, 2002

[2] *Harry Potter and the Order of the Phoenix.* J.K. Rowling. Scholastic Inc., 2003 page 530.

[3] *Morristown Daily Record.* Section E, Health & Fitness. Tuesday, February 15, 2005. Brandi Stafford/Gannett Newspapers. Ellen S. Wilkowe, staff writer.

Suggested Reading

Ackerman, Diane – *A Natural History of the Senses*. New York, Vintage Books. a division of Random House Inc, 1990.

Alpert, Richard. *Be Here Now*. Hanuman Foundation, 1971: Distributed by Crown Publishing Co., New York, NY.

Antoninus, Marcus Aurelius, *The Meditations of Marcus Aurelius Antoninus*. Dover Publications Inc., 1997.

Campbell, Joseph. *The Hero With A Thousand Faces*. New York: Barnes & Noble, Published and arranged with Princeton University by Fine Communications New York.

Coelho, Paulo – *The Alchemist*. Harper Collins, New York: 1998

De Saint-Exupery, Antoine. *The Little Prince*. New York: Harcourt, Brace and Company, 1943.

Frydman, Maurice – "I Am That," *Talks with SRI NISARGADATTA MAHARAJ.* Durham, North Carolina. The Acorn Press 1988.

Hesse, Herman. *Siddhartha* Bantam Books 1922.

Hyde, Lewis W. *The Gift, Imagination and the Erotic Life of Property.* New York: Vintage Books a div of Random House Inc, 1979.

Jones, Charlie and Doran, Kim. *Be the Ball-Golf Instruction Book for the Mind.* 2000, Andrew McMeel Publishing, Kansas City Missouri.

Jung, C.G. *The Basic Writings Of C.G Young – Memories, Dreams, Reflections.* New York: The Modern Library, Random House, Inc 1959.

Klein, Jean – *The Ease of Being.* Acorn Press, 1984.

Krishnamurti, J – Total Freedom. Harper Collins, New York., 1996

Lannoy, Richard – *ANANDAMAYI, her Life and Wisdom.* London Element Books LTD, 1996.

Mancini, Anna *The Intelligence of Dreams.* Buenos Books America, Delaware: 2002.

Muktananda, Swami – *From the Finite to the Infinite, Parts I and II.* South Fallsburg, New York, SYDA Foundation 1989.

Nietzsche, Friedrich Wilhelm. *Human All Too Human.* University of Nebraska Press, Lincoln, NE: First Bison Books Printing 1996.

Satchitananda, Swami – *To Know Yourself: The Essential Teachings of Swami SATCHITANANDA.* Shakticom, Integral Yoga Communication.

Watts, Alan – *ZEN the Supreme Experience.* Mark Watts, ed. Vega 2002.

Yogananda, Paramahansa. *Autobiography of a YOGI.* New York: The Philosophical Library, Inc. 1946.

In three words, I can sum up everything I've learned about life: it goes on.

Robert Frost

Also published by Buenos Books America:

Maat Revealed, Philosophy of Justice in Ancient Egypt, by Anna Mancini Ph. D

E-Book: 5.50 USD ISBN 9781932848113
Paperback: 16.95 USD ISBN 9781932848106
http://www.buenosbooks.us/maat.html

LaVergne, TN USA
16 March 2011
220472LV00002B/10/A